PRAYERS
for Every Day

Publications International, Ltd.

Dates to Remember

_____   _____

_____   _____

_____   _____

_____   _____

_____   _____

_____   _____

_____   _____

Cover photo: Shutterstock.com

Interior photos: American Spirit Images, Art Explosion, Artville, Getty, Shutterstock.com

Unless otherwise marked, scripture quotations are taken from *The Holy Bible, King James Version*. Copyright © 1977, 1984, Thomas Nelson, Inc., Publishers.

Scripture quotations marked NRSV are taken from the *New Revised Standard Version* of the Bible. Copyright © 1989 by the Division of Christian Education of the National Council of the Churches of Christ in the USA. Used by permission. All rights reserved.

Copyright © 2014 Publications International, Ltd. All rights reserved. This book may not be reproduced or quoted in whole or in part by any means whatsoever without written permission from:

Louis Weber, CEO
Publications International, Ltd.
7373 North Cicero Avenue
Lincolnwood, Illinois 60712

Permission is never granted for commercial purposes.

ISBN: 978-1-4508-8982-7

Manufactured in China.

Anniversary Gifts

First:	Paper	**Thirteenth:**	Lace
Second:	Cotton	**Fourteenth:**	Ivory
Third:	Leather	**Fifteenth:**	Crystal
Fourth:	Fruit/flowers	**Twentieth:**	China
Fifth:	Wood	**Twenty-fifth:**	Silver
Sixth:	Candy/iron	**Thirtieth:**	Pearls
Seventh:	Wool/copper	**Thirty-fifth:**	Coral
Eighth:	Bronze/pottery	**Fortieth:**	Ruby
Ninth:	Pottery/willow	**Forty-fifth:**	Sapphire
Tenth:	Tin/aluminum	**Fiftieth:**	Gold
Eleventh:	Steel	**Fifty-fifth:**	Emerald
Twelfth:	Silk/linen	**Sixtieth:**	Diamond

To:

_____

From:

_____

December

Birthdays & Anniversaries

_____   _____
_____   _____
_____   _____
_____   _____
_____   _____
_____   _____
_____   _____
_____   _____

Birthstone: Turquoise   Flower: Poinsettia

Photo credits: **American Spirit Images:** February 11; **Art Explosion:** May 4; July 8; September 30; November 28; **Artville:** April 7, 8; October 13, 19, 20, 29; December 28; **Getty:** January 2, 3, 4, 8, 10, 12, 13, 15, 16, 17, 18, 29; February 6, 8, 15, 27; March 10, 11, 15, 16, 18, 28; April 1, 2, 3, 4, 5, 9, 10; May 1, 7, 9, 20, 26, 27, 28, 29; June 6, 7, 23, 25; July 16, 30, 31; August 1, 2, 3, 6, 8, 11, 12, 14, 15, 17, 18, 21; September 5, 7, 8, 10, 21, 26; October 7, 14, 15, 16, 18, 22, 23, 25, 26; November 4, 20, 21, 26, 27, 30; December 1, 2, 4, 6, 11, 13, 16, 19, 20, 21, 23, 25, 26, 27, 31; **Shutterstock.com:** January 7, 6, 9, 14, 22, 26, 28, 31; February 2, 3, 5, 7, 10, 12, 17, 19, 21, 23, 25; March 1, 2, 4, 5, 6, 7, 9, 12, 13, 14, 17, 21, 22, 23, 25, 29, 30, 31; April 11, 19, 20, 21, 23, 24; May 5, 14, 15, 18, 21, 31; June 1, 2, 3, 4, 13, 14, 15, 17, 18, 19, 20, 21, 22, 24, 29, 30; July 1, 2, 3, 5, 6, 7, 9, 10, 12, 13, 14, 15, 18, 19, 21, 22, 23, 24, 25, 28; August 7, 16, 20, 25, 27, 30; September 1, 3, 6, 9, 12, 13, 14, 15, 17, 19, 20, 23, 27, 28, 29, 30; October 5, 8, 10, 11, 27; November 5, 7, 8, 10, 13, 15, 16, 18, 22, 24, 25; December 5, 9, 10, 12 15, 17

November

Birthdays & Anniversaries

_____   _____

_____   _____

_____   _____

_____   _____

_____   _____

_____   _____

_____   _____

Birthstone: Topaz   Flower: Chrysanthemum

January 1

The slate is clean, Lord, the calendar as bare as the Christmas tree. Bless the New Year that beckons. I sing of you as help in ages past but need to know you as hope for years to come. Help me face what I must, celebrate every triumph I can, and make any changes I need.

October
Birthdays & Anniversaries

_____   _____
_____   _____
_____   _____
_____   _____
_____   _____
_____   _____
_____   _____

Birthstone: Opal   Flower: Dahlia

January 2

Why is there so much pain in the world, God? It's so hard to understand. Lord, help me through it all. Help me comprehend or at least simply trust in you.

September
Birthdays & Anniversaries

_____   _____
_____   _____
_____   _____
_____   _____
_____   _____
_____   _____
_____   _____
_____   _____

Birthstone: Sapphire   Flower: Aster

January 3

Remember not the sins of my youth, nor my transgressions: according to thy mercy remember thou me for thy goodness' sake, O Lord.

Psalm 25:7

August
Birthdays & Anniversaries

_____   _____
_____   _____
_____   _____
_____   _____
_____   _____
_____   _____
_____   _____
_____   _____

Birthstone: Peridot   Flower: Gladiolus

January 4

Today I need your help, God. I'm feeling the need for a breath of fresh air. The old habits and attitudes I've clung to for so long seem stale. Renew me from the inside out, starting now.

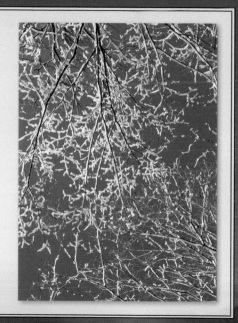

July
Birthdays & Anniversaries

_____   _____

_____   _____

_____   _____

_____   _____

_____   _____

_____   _____

_____   _____

Birthstone: Ruby   Flower: Sweet Pea

January 5

Lord, behold our family here assembled.
We thank you this place in which we dwell,
for the love that unites us, for the peace
accorded us this day, for the hope with which
we expect the morrow; for the health, the
work, the food and the bright skies that make
our lives delightful; for our friends in all
parts of the earth. Amen.

Robert Louis Stevenson

June
Birthdays & Anniversaries

_____   _____
_____   _____
_____   _____
_____   _____
_____   _____
_____   _____
_____   _____
_____   _____

Birthstone: Pearl   Flower: Rose

$\mathcal{L}$ord, help me not to be stubborn. I want my broken heart to heal. Amen.

May
Birthdays & Anniversaries

_____ _____
_____ _____
_____ _____
_____ _____
_____ _____
_____ _____
_____ _____

Birthstone: Emerald   Flower: Lily of the Valley

January 7

Gentle healers of mind, body, and spirit are surely a gift from you sent to travel lonely roads as companions. Sustain them; they are a channel of your love.

April
Birthdays & Anniversaries

_____   _____

_____   _____

_____   _____

_____   _____

_____   _____

_____   _____

_____   _____

Birthstone: Diamond   Flower: Daisy or Lily

January 8

$\mathcal{Y}$ea, though I walk through the valley of the shadow of death, I will fear no evil: for thou art with me; thy rod and thy staff they comfort me.

Psalm 23:4

March
Birthdays & Anniversaries

_____

_____

_____

_____

_____

_____

_____

Birthstone: Aquamarine   Flower: Violet

*L*et me know the satisfaction of forgiving today, O Lord. I have held my peace, doused my anger. Now it is time to extend my hand.

February
Birthdays & Anniversaries

_____   _____

_____   _____

_____   _____

_____   _____

_____   _____

_____   _____

_____   _____

Birthstone: Amethyst   Flower: Primrose

January 10

God, bless me in my solitude. I know that my character is what I am in the dark, when no one is watching me.

January
Birthdays & Anniversaries

_____   _____

_____   _____

_____   _____

_____   _____

_____   _____

_____   _____

_____   _____

Birthstone: Garnet   Flower: Carnation

January 11

God, make me an open vessel through which the waters of your Spirit flow freely. Let your love move through me and out into my world, touching everyone I come in contact with. Express your joy through the special talents you have given me, that others may come to know your presence in their own lives by witnessing your presence in mine. Amen.

December 31

*H*eavenly Father, give us the forgiving spirit we so badly need to heal the wounds of the past. Help us live "the better life" by making peace with our enemies and understanding that they, too, need your love. Amen.

January 12

*H*ow can we recognize any of your needful ones we are to feed, clothe, and tend, Lord, when we see menace in every outstretched hand? Inspire and help us reclaim our world for living in, not hiding from.

O God, I want to leave
a legacy of goodness!

January 13

How precious also are thy thoughts unto me,
O God! how great is the sum of them!

Psalm 139:17

December 29

Savior, like a shepherd lead us,
Much we need thy tender care;
In thy pleasant pastures feed us,
For our use thy folds prepare.
Blessed Jesus, blessed Jesus,
Thou hast bought us, thine we are.
Blessed Jesus, blessed Jesus,
Thou hast bought us, thine we are.

Dorothy A. Thrupp

January 14

Lord, either lighten my burden or strengthen my back.

Thomas Fuller

December 28

$\mathcal{B}$lessed Creator,
thank you for the
loving people in my
life. Thank you for their
open hearts and minds.
Thank you for making
them like you. Amen.

January 15

Give me the tools for building peace, O God, when tempers flare. Needed tools include a kind of heart and faith that measures each tiny rebuilt bridge a triumph.

December 27

$\mathcal{I}$n this day of bigger is best, Lord, I wonder what difference my little light can make. Remind me of the laser, so tiny, yet when it is focused, it has infinite power. This little light of mine, O Lord, give it such focus.

January 16

*H*eavenly Father, your grace can refresh and renew me with the living water of hope and faith. Please help mc livc fully the life you have given me. Amen.

December 26

$\mathcal{T}$hou art worthy, O Lord, to receive glory and honour and power: for thou hast created all things, and for thy pleasure they are and were created.

Revelation 4:11

January 17

Lord, I know that doubts and confusion don't come from you. On days when everything I know to be true is challenged—and I feel like I'm walking through a fog that won't lift—be my source of truth and light. Bring me back to complete trust in you.

December 25

Today I celebrate the birth of your Son, my Lord and Savior, Jesus Christ. I celebrate this Christmas with hope, with peace, and with joy. Through your giving my life is secure. Through your love I, too, can give love. You are the source of my being.

January 18

The steps of a good man are ordered by the Lord: and he delighteth in his way. Though he fall, he shall not be utterly cast down: for the Lord upholdeth him with his hand.

Psalm 37:23–24

December 24

*L*oving Father, help me remember the birth of Jesus, that I may share in the song of the angels, the gladness of the shepherds, and the wisdom of the wise men. Close the door of hate and open the door of love all over the world. Let kindness come with every gift and good desires with every greeting.

January 19

There is every reason to give up and give in, steadfast God, for days are a struggling drudgery. When I falter, remind me that with you I am as resilient as crocuses blooming in the snow.

December 23

*E*ven though I walk through the darkest valley, I fear no evil; for you are with me; your rod and your staff— they comfort me.

-Psalm 23:4 NRSV

January 20

Lord, if we could see the future, it would be easy to have hope. Real hope is when we can't see the end of the road, but still trust you to lead us there.

December 22

Encircle me in the arms of your love.
Fill me with your perfect peace.
Though my soul faints,
Sustain me through hope in your word.

January 21

Thine, O Lord is the greatness, and the power, and the glory, and the victory, and the majesty: for all that is in the heaven and in the earth is thine; thine is the kingdom, O Lord, and thou art exalted as head above all.

1 Chronicles 29:11

I can relax, O Lord of light, during these darkest days of winter, knowing that in order for trees to blossom and bear fruit and the maple tree to yield its sugar, a resting stillness of dormancy is a welcome part of growth.

January 22

*F*ather, you help me to live gracefully by blessing me with wonderful friends. Thank you for making them as good as you are. Amen.

December 20

The day is thine, the night also is thine: thou hast prepared the light and the sun. Thou hast set all the borders of the earth: thou hast made summer and winter.

Psalm 74:16–17

January 23

O God of rest and
rejuvenation, guide me
to find ways to let your
nurturing reach me. I need
to be healthy and well
rested in order to provide,
lead, and inspire.

December 19

Worries are hard to dismiss, Lord. They seem to grow bigger and bigger until they take over my life. Please help me conquer them, one at a time. Your reassurance is welcome. Amen.

January 24

I want to belong and go to great lengths to fit anonymously in, forgetting that your people are like snowflakes, no two, thank God, alike. Each snowflake and child of yours is the same in essence but different in form. Bless my unique, one-of-a-kind value. I am heartened to know that no one is created more special. It is not your way to make one snowflake, or one person, better than another.

December 18

Lord, I want to live life to its fullest. And although I know I shouldn't place my own wants before others' wants, it is so easy to think my dreams for the future matter most. Remind me to make compromises. Love can get me further in life than selfishness. Amen.

January 25

*L*ife, once filled with sunlight and promise, has been colored by loss and is now all storm and shadow. Use my tears, Lord, as the showers needed to bring rainbows. Shine your love on me as the sun; lift my eyes so I can see even the smallest curves of hope in the dark (lightening) sky.

December 17

 I am weak, but thou art mighty; hold me with thy powerful hand.

William Williams

January 26

$\mathcal{T}$each me to do thy will; for thou art my God: thy spirit is good; lead me into the land of uprightness.

Psalm 143:10

December 16

$\mathcal{L}$ord, the clamor of my life seems unbearable. There are people pressing in on all sides, decisions crying out to be made, and problems to be solved. I struggle to get out of bed in the morning. I want to hide. Please help me in these times of need.

January 27

Almighty God, my faith in you is undergirded by your faithfulness. No matter how many times I turn away, you patiently wait for me to return to you. Instill in me that same sense of honor and faithfulness that is yours, Lord. May I be as faithful to you as you have been to me.

December 15

My lips shall greatly rejoice when I sing unto thee;
and my soul, which thou hast redeemed.

Psalm 71:23

January 28

Faith is the substance of things hoped for,
the evidence of things not seen.

Hebrews 11:1

O Holy Creator, who hath bound together heaven and earth, let me walk through your kingdom comforted and protected by the warm rays of your love. Let me be healed as I stand basking in the divine light of your presence, where strength and hope and joy are found. Let me sit at rest in the valley of your peace, surrounded by the fortress of your loving care.

$\mathcal{G}$od Almighty, please help me to put everything into perspective. I want to be realistic but also optimistic. Please send me hope and give me strength of mind to make things right again. Amen.

December 13

*F*or great is your love, reaching to the heavens.

Psalm 57:10

January 30

If I am right, Thy grace impart,
Still in the right to stay;
If I am wrong, oh teach my heart
To find that better way.

Alexander Pope

December 12

Thank you, God, for the wisdom to know when to speak, what to say, and how to say it. Guard my mouth today from any form of foolishness, that in all circumstances I might honor you with my words.

January 31

*H*eavenly Father, I am
glad to have even just
one companion, but
you have sent me many
more! I thank you for
my friends and family.
I am happy to have
so many shoulders on
which I can lean. Amen.

December 11

Temptations are
everywhere, God.
Please stay nearby
and keep me strong.

February 1

Ah, what solace
there is in your promise
of peace. True help
and real peace are to
be found from trusting
in your guidance and
inspiration.

Lord, how many lives have been changed by the reforming, transforming power of your Word! So often I stumble upon a common verse, and it strikes me in a new, wonderful way. It brings breathtaking clarity when I need it most. Thank you for giving us your Word, Lord. We would be lost without it.

February 2

I know that my true colors are revealed when no one else can see. Because temptation is the greatest here, the possibility of a setback looms large.

December 9

Lord, thou hast been our dwelling place in all generations.

Psalm 90:1

February 3

$\mathcal{B}$e merciful unto me, O God, be merciful unto me: for my soul trusteth in thee: yea, in the shadow of thy wings will I make refuge, until these calamities be overpast.

Psalm 57:1

Holy Spirit, the life that gives life.
You are the cause of all movement;
You are the breath of all creatures;
You are the salve that purifies our souls;
You are the ointment that heals our wounds;
You are the fire that warms our hearts;
You are the light that guides our feet.
Let all the world praise you.

Hildegard of Bingen

O Word of God Incarnate,
O Wisdom from on high,
O Truth unchanged, unchanging,
O Light of our dark sky:
We praise thee for the radiance
That from the hallowed page,
A lantern to our footsteps,
Shines on from age to age.

O Word of God Incarnate

December 7

$\mathscr{I}$ have such good intentions, Lord of promise, but sometimes I slip in carrying them out. Guide my actions so that they match my words as I make footprints for others to follow. Make me worthy of being a pathfinder. Amen.

February 5

I praise you, Lord, for eternal life. And I thank you for your everlasting love of me. Amen.

December 6

Slow my pell-mell race into the future, everlasting God, for I am racing past the exquisite moment, which, like a snowflake, is unlike any other and never to be retrieved.

February 6

$\mathcal{A}$ chart of my efforts to change traces a jagged course, Lord, like the lines on a heart-rate monitor. Reassure me that instead of measuring my failures, ups and downs mean simply that I am alive and ever-changing. Help me become consistent, but deliver me from flat lines.

December 5

If any of you lack wisdom, let him ask of God, that giveth to all men liberally, and upbraideth not; and it shall be given him.

James 1:5

February 7

I call upon you, for you will answer me, O God;
incline your ear to me, hear my words.

Psalm 17:6 NRSV

December 4

Father, nothing moves me more to love others than reflecting on how you love me. I think of all the things you could have held against me and used as reasons to not love me. And yet you always look for ways to forgive, restore our relationship, and move forward. I want to love like that!

February 8

$\mathcal{D}$ear Lord, if I am to succeed meaningfully in this life, I must succeed first in being a person rich in integrity and love. Only then will all other successes find their significance. I know this is true because you've told me this so many times in the past. Please continue to help me be the person you want me to be. Amen.

December 3

Angel of God, my guardian dear,
To whom God's love commits me here,
Ever this day, be at my side,
To light and guard, rule and guide.
Amen.

Traditional Prayer

February 9

O God, your love is so great. I'm not sure
that I can love as you do or even love others
in a way that will please you. God, teach me
how to really love my family, my friends,
and even strangers. I trust in the power
of your love to make me into a far more
loving person than I am today. Amen.

December 2

$\mathcal{D}$ear God, it's not fair.
It's hard for me to believe
that whatever happens
is okay. I want to feel
your presence, even if
you don't offer a miracle.
Please understand how I
feel and give me hope.
Amen.

February 10

When I doubt
your miracle-making
power, Lord, show
me the ordinary
miracles of seasons,
of hope regained, and
of love from family
and friends.

There's so much to be grateful for in this life! Thank you, God, for Your many blessings.

February 11

*L*ife has made even the most hopeful people skeptical, Lord of truth. Much is bogus, and I am uncertain. Thank you for the gift of doubt, for it sparks my seeking. Keep me lively and excited as I set off on quests blessed by you, heeding your advice to knock, seek, ask.

November 30

Inspired by you, Great God, and grateful for the unique gifts I am discovering, I toss myself into the stream of life to make ripples wherever I am. In your hands, my gifts can offer a gift that keeps on making ever-widening circles to reach all those stranded on shore.

February 12

Mine enemies would daily swallow me up: for they be many that fight against me, O thou most High. What time I am afraid, I will trust in thee. In God I will praise his word, in God I have put my trust; I will not fear what flesh can do unto me.

Psalm 56:2–4

Teach us, good Lord, to serve Thee as Thou deservest. To give and not to count the cost: To fight and not to heed the wounds: To toil and not to seek for rest: To labour and not to ask for any reward save that of knowing that we do thy will.

St. Ignatius Loyola

O God, giver of all good things, my faith in you is like a treasure to be mined—it sustains, it inspires, and it provides me with unimagined contentment.

November 28

God, you love me more than I can ever comprehend. You have even given your angels charge over me, to guide and protect me. Help me be worthy of your love and the angels' care, and that those I meet might consider me as a bearer of angelic love.

February 14

On Valentine's Day, God, I think of the love of my life. I am convinced that your love is reflected through our love. I am truly privileged to have such a special relationship. Thank you, God.

God, encouragement through friends and family lifts my heart just as sunshine turns roses skyward. May their love inspire me to stretch my soul toward the warmth and nurture of your radiant affection for me.

February 15

In my distress I cried unto the Lord, and he heard me.

Psalm 120:1

November 26

$\mathcal{L}$ord of abundant life, I am humbled by my bounty. I have so much more than I need. Help me share my good fortune. I give the heartiest thanks for your diligent, steadfast care.

February 16

Comfort, dear God, those whose eyes are filled with tears and those whose backs are near breaking with the weight of a heavy burden. Heal those with wounded hearts and whose faith has been dealt a blow. Bless all who mourn and despair. Help those who can't imagine how they'll make it through another day. For your goodness and mercy are enough for all the troubles in the world. Amen.

November 25

Let the heaven and earth praise him, the seas,
and every thing that moveth therein.

Psalm 69:34

February 17

*O*pen wide the window
of our spirits, O Lord,
and fill us full of light;
Open wide the door of
our hearts, that we may
receive and entertain
thee with all our powers
of adoration and love.

Christina Rossetti

November 24

God, please help me to accept your itinerary for my life's journey no matter where it brings me. I will wait for you to decide when I should return to your home. Amen.

February 18

Seeking courage, Lord, I bundle my
fears and place them in your hands.
Too heavy for me, too weighty even to
ponder in this moment,
such shadowy terrors shrink to size in
my mind and—how wonderful!—
wither to nothing in your grasp.

November 23

Lord, far too often I try to steer the course of my life without consulting you, and I always run into problems. Set me on a true course that will bring me closer to you. Amen.

February 19

Let the words of my mouth, and the meditation of my heart, be acceptable in thy sight, O Lord, my strength, and my redeemer.

Psalm 19:14

November 22

Hear my prayer, O God;
give ear to the words of my mouth.

Psalm 54:2

February 20

O Lord, I blew it again. Help me know that wringing my hands in the wake of failure is as useless as lamenting storm-felled trees. Give me eyes to see beyond chaos to possibilities. In that way, I won't miss finding out what could happen if I picked up a saw and took it to that tree, making firewood around which friends can gather.

November 21

*S*ource of all life and love,
let this family be a place of
warmth on a cold night, a
friendly haven for the lonely
stranger, a small sanctuary
of peace in the midst of
swirling activity. Above
all, let its members seek to
reflect the kindness of your
own heart, day by day.

$\mathcal{D}$ear God, help me
start anew. Teach me
how to heal by learning
new ways to live. Amen.

November 20

*L*ord, please be my strength. When I am scared, please make me brave. When I am unsteady, please bring your stability to me. I look to your power for an escape from pain. I welcome your comfort. Amen.

February 22

*H*eavenly Father, you are the author of love. I am able to love only because you first loved me. You taught me how to love you and others. I want everyone to know your perfect love, and I invite the fragrance of your love to permeate my home.

November 19

I will love thee, O Lord, my strength. The Lord is my rock, and my fortress, and my deliverer; my God, my strength, in whom I will trust; my buckler, and the horn of my salvation, and my high tower.

Psalm 18:1–2

February 23

$\mathcal{D}$ear God, show me ways to help your hurting, needful world. I need to see that I am not helpless or hopeless but that all efforts, small as they might seem, can matter.

We don't really know why
we have to get sick, Lord.
We only know your promise:
No matter where we are or
what we are called to endure,
there you are in the midst of
it with us, never leaving our
side. Not for a split second.
Thank you, Lord of all.

February 24

Lord, thou hast heard the desire of the humble: thou wilt prepare their heart, thou wilt cause thine ear to hear: To judge the fatherless and the oppressed, that the man of the earth may no more oppress.

Psalm 10:17–18

Dear Lord and Father of humankind,
Forgive our foolish ways;
Reclothe us in our rightful mind,
In purer lives Thy service find,
In deeper reverence, praise.

John Greenleaf Whittier

February 25

I need you, God, in all the seasons of my life. I need your angels gathered around me. I need to believe you care for me in all my ages and stages. Give me the faith that reminds me I don't have to go it alone. Bless me with whispers of angels in my life, until the end of my days.

My guard is constant and vigilant, protecting me against the next episode of my humanness. I know to err is human, but why so often? Peace only comes, God of wholeness, through reassurance that with you, mistakes, errors—even disasters—can yield treasures. I am so grateful.

February 26

I believe, God, that you give us faith as a means of getting in touch with your love. For once we have that love, we can pass it on to others.

Henry Drummond

November 15

$\mathcal{B}$ut I have trusted in thy mercy; my heart shall rejoice in thy salvation. I will sing unto the Lord, because he hath dealt bountifully with me.

Psalm 13:5–6

February 27

Heavenly Father, it is good to
remember that everything that
lives and breathes is sacred to
you. I must never feel superior
to any other human being—for
we are all precious in your eyes.
You have given life to all, and
I must make the choices that
lead to kindness and peace.
You created us, but how we live
together is up to us. Thank you.

November 14

God, sometimes I wish I could be saved from the struggle and pain of learning the hard way. But, Lord, that's not your plan, and I need to be willing to wait as you work gently from the inside out. Please grant me some strength in this time of uncertainty. I trust and love you. Amen.

February 28

*H*eal me, O Lord, and I shall be healed; save me,
and I shall be saved: for thou art my praise.

Jeremiah 17:14

November 13

Continue in prayer, and watch in the same with thanksgiving.

Colossians 4:2

February 29

Lord, give me your compassion today. When I look at the people around me, help me to see them through your eyes. I know you love us all equally, Lord. And you love us completely and unconditionally. May I compassionately reach out to others in your name today.

November 12

$\mathcal{G}$od, I pray for the strength and the wisdom to know what to do in this situation. I pray for enough love to forgive this person for the pain they have caused me and to forgive myself for the ill will I have harbored against this person. Help me be a truly forgiving person so that the weight of resentment may be lifted from my shoulders. Amen.

March 1

My trust is in you, God of
miracles and surprises, for
daily I feel your presence
in a dozen ways.

November 11

Watchful God,
thank you for those
persons in uniform who
have watched over us and
cared for us. Bless them,
guide them in their duties,
and keep them safe.

March 2

But I trusted in thee, O Lord: I said, Thou art my God. My times are in thy hand: deliver me from the hand of mine enemies, and from them that persecute me.

Psalm 31:14–15

November 10

God, hear my prayer. Bless me with patience and a steadfast heart to help me through such emotionally trying times. Heal the wounds of my heart and soul with the soothing balm of your comforting presence, that I may be able to love and to live again.

March 3

Move our hearts with the calm, smooth flow of your grace. Let the river of your love run through our souls. May my soul be carried by the current of your love, towards the wide, infinite ocean of heaven. Stretch out my heart with your strength, as you stretch out the sky above the earth. Smooth out any wrinkles of hatred or resentment. Enlarge my soul that it may know more fully your truth.

Gilbert of Hoyland

November 9

$\mathcal{Y}$ou call me to courage,
Lord, but incrementally, as
a child emboldened to walk
along placing each small
foot in larger footprints.
As I am following you, you
show me a path marked out
that leads to safety.

Mercy is a beautiful word, Father. I breathe a sigh of relief just thinking about your mercy toward me. Help me to remember that—as the recipient of such generous forgiveness—I should be quick to forgive others, whether I am the victim of a minor thoughtless slight or some bigger affront.

November 8

Bless my family, Lord. They are a gift from you, evidence of your unwillingness for me to be alone. Until I see you face to face, may the faces of those I love be to me as your own.

March 5

I have not hid thy righteousness within my heart;
I have declared thy faithfulness and thy salvation:
I have not concealed thy lovingkindness and thy
truth from the great congregation.

Psalm 40:10

November 7

Blessed be the name of God for ever and ever:
for wisdom and might are his.

Daniel 2:20

March 6

$\mathcal{L}$ord, I don't like to let stress destroy my even keel, but sometimes it does. I need your wisdom to help me manage the load and your grace to keep me from being ill-tempered.

November 6

God, shine your healing light down upon me today, for my path is filled with painful obstacles and my suffering fogs my vision. Clear the challenges from the road I must walk upon, or at least walk with me as I confront them. With you, I know I can endure anything. With you, I know I can make it through to the other side, where joy awaits. Amen.

$\mathcal{G}$od, I know that you close some doors in my life in order to open new ones. I know that things change and come to an end in order to leave room for new beginnings. Help me have the boldness and enthusiasm to let go of the old and accept the new. Amen.

November 5

Bless you, Lord! The heavens declare your glory; the skies proclaim your mighty power. And here I am, looking up into those vast regions, knowing that the tiniest cell in my body is a most glorious miracle, as well. Bless you, Lord!

March 8

Thy mercy, O Lord, is in the heavens;
and thy faithfulness reacheth unto the
clouds. Thy righteousness is like the great
mountains; thy judgments are a great deep:
O Lord, thou preservest man and beast.
How excellent is thy lovingkindness, O God!
therefore the children of men put their trust
under the shadow of thy wings.

Psalm 36:5–7

November 4

Trust in the Lord with all thine heart;
and lean not unto thine own understanding.

Proverbs 3:5

March 9

*B*less me with silent conversations, O God, so I may be with you while doing chores, while singing in the shower, while brushing the cat. Sometimes words don't have to be spoken to be understood, and I get your message, too, in the silence that fills and comforts.

November 3

Dear Lord, I live in a broken world. Heal me of my prejudices, sicknesses, compulsions, hatreds, and shortsightedness. Help me to see people as you see them. Teach me to treat life as the gift you meant it to be. Give me love to spare and forgiveness that can only come from you. Amen.

March 10

Help me cast aside my old worn-out ways so that I can begin again. Renew me from the inside out, Lord.

November 2

Lord, perfect for me what is lacking of thy gifts; of faith, help thou mine unbelief; of hope, establish my trembling hope; of love, kindle its smoking flax.

Lancelot Andrewes

March 11

*J*esus, Teacher of patience, Pattern of gentleness,
Prophet of the kingdom of heaven, I adore Thee.

A Book of Prayers for Students

November 1

I cannot wander so far in any direction, vigilant God, that you are not already there.

March 12

$\mathcal{D}$ear Father God, you sent your son to be my Lord, to watch over me, to bring me comfort, strength, hope, and healing when my heart is broken and my life seems shattered. I will never be alone, not when you are here with me always and forever. Remind me to look to you for strength. Amen.

October 31

Amidst hobgoblins and pranksters, O God, I seek a quiet corner this autumn evening to give thanks for the saints whose day this really is. Remind me of the pillars upon which my faith rests today. Keep the trick-or-treating fun, clean, and safe and my faith memories aware, for it is too easy to lose track of what I really celebrate in the darkness of this night.

Calm me enough,
O Lord, to breathe deeply and
restoratively. Prayer restores
me in the presence of all that
threatens to undo me, which
I name to you now.

$\mathcal{R}$ejoice, and be exceeding glad:
for great is your reward in heaven.

Matthew 5:12

March 14

Lord, I know it isn't enough to experience love. I have to get out there in the world and do loving things as well. Help me find ways to be of service and bring more love into my life. Direct the course of my actions, and inspire me with ideas that help me, in turn, inspire others. Amen.

October 29

Standing today, O God, upon sturdy ancestral roots that knew you as the Source of Life, I feel the need to thank all who came before me and to drop to my knees in gratitude to you.

March 15

*E*nliven my imagination, God of new life, so that I can see through today's troubles to coming newness. Surround me with your caring so that I can live as if the new has already begun.

October 28

It is good, dear God, to be a part of this family: circle of love, place of rest, bastion of peace. When every other source of comfort fails, this is where I return. Thank you for being in our midst.

Lord, grant me a simple,
kind, open, believing,
loving and generous heart,
worthy of being your
dwelling place.

John Sergieff

October 27

$\mathcal{H}$elp me take stock of your gifts to me, Lord. I'm good at things that appear to be so insignificant. Chances are you can use any one of them, no matter how simple it appears, to help others. Remind me that it's not what I do but my doing that ultimately matters.

March 17

Bless to me, O God, the earth beneath my feet,
Bless to me, O God, the path whereon I go,
Bless to me, O God, the people whom I meet,
Today, tonight and tomorrow.

Celtic Blessing

October 26

Remember, O Lord, thy tender mercies and thy lovingkindnesses; for they have been ever of old.

Psalm 25:6

March 18

The Lord will strengthen him upon the bed of
languishing: thou wilt make all his bed in his sickness.

Psalm 41:3

October 25

*D*ear God, hear my prayer. I am suffering and in need of your merciful blessings. Please take me into your arms. Give me the courage to keep going through difficult times and the fortitude to move beyond the outer illusions of pain and despair. Only you can heal me, God. Amen.

My closest friends, dear Lord, are a reprieve for my soul. Their acceptance sets me free to be myself. Their unconditional love forgives my failings. Thank you for these people who are a reflection of your love in my life. Help me be a friend who will lay down my life in such loving ways.

October 24

*J*esus, friend of the poor,
Feeder of the hungry,
Healer of the sick,
I adore thee.

A Book of Prayers for Students

I pray that you may have the power to comprehend, with all the saints, what is the breadth and length and height and depth, and to know the love of Christ that surpasses knowledge, so that you may be filled with all the fullness of God.

Ephesians 3:18–19 NRSV

October 23

$\mathcal{G}$od, I usually blame you first when things go wrong. Forgive me for even considering that you would deliberately hurt one of your very own children. What could you possibly have to gain? Thank you for your presence, and please forgive my many sins.

March 21

$\mathcal{D}$ear Lord, thank you for healing my heart and bringing joy and meaning back into my life. Thank you for the people who truly care for me. Help mc bc a soothing and joyful presence in their lives as well. Amen.

October 22

Dear Lord, when I am sad, you give me hope. When I am lost, you offer me direction and guidance. When I am alone, you stand beside me. When my heart aches with sorrow, you bring me new blessings. Thank you for your gifts of grace, of love, and of healing. Amen.

March 22

Spirit, carry me like a
feather upon the current
to a place of serenity. Let
the waters flow over me
like cleansing balm. Set me
upon the dry place, where
life begins anew. Spirit,
carry me like a feather
back home again.

October 21

When life goes awry, Lord, I point the finger at you. Heaven help me, I want it both ways: you as sender and fixer of trouble. Help me know you don't will trouble. And when the good you want for me isn't possible in the randomness of life, I know you are with me.

March 23

O give thanks unto the Lord; for he is good: because his mercy endureth for ever.

Psalm 118:1

October 20

Into thine hand I commit my spirit: thou hast redeemed me, O Lord God of truth.

Psalm 31:5

March 24

As storm clouds gathered, Father, I used to run for cover, panicked and picking a favorite escape. None of them worked for long, Dear God, and none of them kept me safe. No more running then. I see it clearly now: Wherever I am standing is a special place, under the shadow of your sheltering wing.

October 19

𝓛ord God, it is hard for me to accept when someone I care about hurts me. I don't want to talk to this person anymore. I consider our friendship to be over. And all because my pride is bruised. Please help me recognize when I am not giving others a chance. Amen.

March 25

Lord, my heart was broken, but I know you can fix it. As I learn to depend on you, give me the same thing you gave your servant David: strength and a song. Amen.

October 18

I get discouraged, O God, my comforter and guide, and feel overwhelmed, which makes me even more discouraged. Lead me beyond negative thoughts and useless circles of worry to a renewed frame of mind. Work your miracle of transformation in me.

March 26

Your son, Jesus, was a reader, Lord.
He read from your own books, the Holy
Scriptures. Books have the power to change.
They can transport us to other places and
other times and can share the wisdom of
the ages. Thank you, Lord, for good books,
especially the Bible, that can show us the
wonder of life in your world.

Be thou my vision, O Lord of my heart;
Naught be all else to me, save that thou art:
Thou my best thought, by day and by night,
Walking or sleeping, thy presence my light.
Riches I heed not, or man's empty praise,
Thou mine inheritance, now and always:
Thou and thou only, first in my heart,
High King of heaven, my treasure thou art.

"Be Thou My Vision"

March 27

$\mathcal{G}$od of Easter surprises, bring back to life friendships faded because of hurt feelings, marriages broken from deceit, love crushed by meanness. In the doing, hope glimmers like dawn's first ray of sun and thaws even the most frozen heart.

October 16

I will freely sacrifice unto thee: I will praise thy name, O Lord; for it is good.

Psalm 54:6

March 28

How grateful I am, God of Knowledge, that you created me so curious. In your wisdom, it is the searcher turning over every leaf who finds four-leaf clovers; the doubter who invents; and the determined, like a duckling pecking its way from the shell, who emerges strong enough to fly.

October 15

*H*eavenly Father, help me examine every passing day in order to find purpose in my life. I want my time to be worthwhile. Remind me to count all my blessings, big and small. Amen.

March 29

*H*appy is that people, that is in such a case:
yea, happy is that people, whose God is the Lord.

Psalm 144:15

Father, unity among your people is precious to you—and precious to us as well. I know unity cannot be achieved without your assistance, though. Help us to keep petty disagreements from dividing us. Give us the grace to work through any disagreement with love and understanding.

March 30

*L*ord, bring me to the place where peace flows like a river, where soft green grasses gently hold the weight of my tired body, where the light of a new sunrise casts warmth.

October 13

Angels surround me with love and protection. Know that they are with me to ease my burden, shield me from evil, lighten my heart, and guide me along my journey.

March 31

You, O Lord, are my refuge. When the days are too full and sleep is hard to come by, I simply need to escape to a quiet place and call on you. In your presence I find strength for my work and peace for my troubled mind. I am grateful for the comfort of your embrace, Lord.

October 12

*Y*es, Father in heaven, often have we found that the world cannot give us peace, O but make us feel that thou art able to give us peace; let us know the truth of thy promise: that the whole world may not be able to take away thy peace.

Soren Kierkegaard

The Lord hath done great things for us; whereof we are glad.

Psalm 126:3

God, grant me the courage to let go of shame, guilt, and anger. Free me of all negative energies, for only then will I become a conduit for joy and a channel for goodness. Amen.

A sturdy bridge, prayer connects me to you, God, and you are always first to celebrate my joys and first to weep at my troubles. It is in this sharing that love brings about its most miraculous ways and I am lifted above the trials and tribulations of life. Thank you, Lord.

October 10

For in thee, O Lord, do I hope: thou wilt hear, O Lord my God.

Psalm 38:15

*H*eavenly Father, your son, Jesus, could have called down heaven to destroy his enemies when he was on earth, but he didn't. Revenge wasn't his mission. Love was. Help me to submit, as he did, to a path of gentleness in the strength of your love. Amen.

God in heaven above,
Bless me with your love.
Send your angel choir to guide me.
Safe within your arms, please hide me.
High in heaven's dome,
I'll make your heart my home.

*J*esus was the fulfillment of
God's promise of salvation.
His life and death made
salvation possible. What
a glorious, selfless gift! I
ponder this blessing every
day, and gratitude and joy
fill my very being.

Lord, thank you for bringing others into my life to help me heal. I appreciate how much they aid me. Please remind me to thank them for reaching out to me. Thank you for extending your love to me through them. Amen.

April 5

Today, O God, I celebrate the rolling away of stones. Remind me, Lord of unexpected appearances, that in this season of spring, rebirth is not so surprising.

October 7

Thou rulest the raging of the sea: when the waves thereof arise, thou stillest them.

Psalm 89:9

O God, we give thanks that your Son Jesus Christ, who has shared our earthly life, has now ascended to prepare our heavenly life. Grant that, through coming to know him by faith on earth, we may come to know him by sight in heaven.

The Gelasian Sacramentary

October 6

$\mathcal{P}$recious Lord, bless me
with your grace that I may
experience the deepest
peace and healing only
you can provide. Show
me the merciful love that
knows no end that I may
rest today knowing I am
cared for. Amen.

April 7

Shall thy wonders be known in the dark? and thy righteousness in the land of forgetfulness?

Psalm 86:12

October 5

$\mathcal{F}$ather, help me to touch and influence others. I want them to recognize and celebrate even the small blessings. I want to surprise them with gestures of love. Amen.

April 8

*J*esus, every time I stop to think of it, I am awed that you provided salvation for us at the price of your own life. Thank you for opening up the way for me to enjoy eternal life with you. May my being be filled with joy, gratitude, and awe at every mention of your name.

$\mathcal{L}$ord, may I be wakeful at sunrise to begin a new day for you, cheerful at sunset for having done my work for you; thankful at moonrise and under starshine for the beauty of the universe. And may I add what little may be in me to your great world.

The Abbot of Greve

April 9

$\mathcal{G}$od, help me listen to those who are wise in the ways of the spirit. Help me hear the inner workings of my own heart. I want to grow closer to you, O God.

October 3

*G*od of my heart, bring
me comfort and peace in
this time of confusion and
sorrow. Help me know
that, although things are
bleak, there is always a
brighter tomorrow.

Lord, I understand that there are and will be problems in my life, but please remind me of your presence when problems seem insurmountable. I want to believe that you know best. I hope to remain patient as I search for purpose. Amen.

O God, stir new possibilities for our vibrant family into life among embers of trust in you. We know the Spirit fans the flame of growth so that we may become one with you, the root from which we, leaf and folk, have their source.

$\mathcal{B}$ut now, O Lord, thou art our father; we are the clay, and thou our potter; and we all are the work of thy hand.

Isaiah 64:8

October 1

This week, give me the wisdom to see my own imperfections clearly and the strength to transform them for the better.

April 12

It takes great courage to heal, Lord, great energy to reach out from this darkness to touch the hem of your garment and ask for healing. Bless the brave voices telling nightmare tales of dreadful wounds to the gifted healers of this world. Together, sufferers and healers are binding up damaged parts and laying down burdens carried so long.

September 30

$\mathcal{B}$ut thou, O Lord, art a shield for me; my glory, and the lifter up of mine head.

Psalm 3:3

April 13

Although the rain still falls, Creator God, it takes such a little bit of sun to create a rainbow, your sign of promise and presence.

September 29

$\mathscr{F}$ather, the wind rustling the leaves reminds me of angel wings all around me. Thank you for such a reminder. Help me stay mindful that the work of angels goes on all the time all around me whether I am aware or not, and that life is even more than I see.

April 14

Lord, in a world where everything seems to be here today and gone tomorrow, how wonderful it is to focus on the rich legacy I have in you. Everything you do and create lasts forever. How reassuring it is to accept that that means I will last forever too. Forever in your kingdom! Thank you, Lord.

September 28

I have been apart and I have lost my way. . . .
And in my hours of darkness when I am not even
sure there is a Thou hearing my call, I still call to
Thee with all my heart. Hear the cry of my voice,
clamoring from this desert, for my soul is parched
and my heart can barely stand this longing.

Gnostic Holy Eucharist

April 15

I am caught up in well-worn, comfy traditions, Lord. Keep them worthy, for like a deer path through the forest, they lead me forward and back. Thank you for the divine love and holiness found in the ordinary.

September 27

Dear God, I know I am not
immune to losing myself
or to hurting others. Please
help me stay on course so
I may find my own true
essence. Amen.

*B*less our homes, dear God, that we
cherish the daily bread before there is none,
discover each other before we leave on our
separate ways, and enjoy each other for
what we are, while we have time to do so.

A Prayer from Hawaii (adapted)

September 26

I cried unto the Lord with my voice, and he heard me out of his holy hill.

Psalm 3:4

Merciful God, my heart is
heavy. Visit me with angels,
that I may receive the peace
that comes only from you.
And then, with the lightness
of angelic wings, may I lift
my face to heaven to receive
your gift of new life.

September 25

*P*rayer, O God, is as steadying as a hand on the rudder of a free-floating boat and as reliable as sunrise after night. It keeps me going, connected as I am to you, the source of wind beneath my daily wings.

April 18

O God, thou art my God; early will I seek thee: my soul thirsteth for thee, my flesh longeth for thee in a dry and thirsty land, where no water is.

Psalm 63:1

September 24

*K*nowing she needs encouragement, I pray for my friend, Lord. Lifting my heart to you on her behalf, may I not fail, either, to reach my hand to hers—just as you are holding mine.

*H*eavenly Father, my diversions seem great. I can't remember when the insurmountable demands started piling up, and I have a hard time seeing the end. Allow me to take a moment from my hectic days to close my eyes and feel your peace. I ask you to lead me. Amen.

September 23

Though I walk in the midst of trouble, thou wilt revive me: thou shalt stretch forth thine hand against the wrath of mine enemies, and thy right hand shall save me.

Psalm 138:7

What a wonderful day! God of rest and peace, I celebrate the joy of ordinary days and rest in your care.

$\mathcal{D}$ear God, I know that I have wronged others over the course of the years. I pray that those moments are long forgotten. If they are not, I pray that I might somehow make them right. I truly forgive anyone who has wronged me, letting go of any grudges or hurt feelings. And I pray that as I forgive, so may I be forgiven. Amen.

April 21

When I feel my control slipping, Lord, I know I only have to call on you for encouragement, direction, and guidance to get your loving assistance.

September 21

Lord, make me an instrument of your peace, where there is hatred, let me sow love; where there is injury, pardon; where there is doubt, faith.

St. Francis of Assisi

*G*od,

Bless the unknown angels who clear the cluttered paths of the lost, who wipe the tears of the grieving, and who hold the hands that tremble in fear. Their names may be known only to you, but their acts of mercy give me the assurance that your love touches everyone, everywhere.

Amen.

September 20

Lord, help us move beyond times when we hurt one another, willingly misunderstand, cherish our differences, assume we know all there is to know about each other, and turn away. Amen.

April 23

God grant me the serenity to accept the things I cannot change, courage to change the things I can, and wisdom to know the difference.

Reinhold Niebuhr

You have said:
We are all one. So
when I am tempted
to separate, alienate,
exasperate my sisters
and brothers, remind
me: We are all one.

*G*od, bless this situation with the gentle, healing power of your love, that I may find the courage to carry on through this dark time of loss and the grace to believe there is happiness ahead. Amen.

September 18

Father, there are many events over which I have no control. However, I do have a choice either to endure trying times or give up. Remind me that the secret of survival is remembering that my hope is in your fairness, goodness, and justice. When I put my trust in you who cannot fail, I can remain faithful. My trust and faithfulness produce the endurance that sees me through the tough times.

$\mathcal{B}$lessed is he whose transgression is forgiven,
whose sin is covered.

Psalm 32:1

Perhaps for just this day, you would help me reach out? Let me bypass these dreads and see instead your hand reaching back to mine—right now—just as it always has.

April 26

When I face difficult hours in my life, hours when in tears I fall to my knees, take the humble offering of my feeble faith and make it strong through your sustaining power.

September 16

It's hard, Lord, to reveal
my heart to you, though it's
the thing I most want to do.
Remind me in this dialogue
that you already know what is
within me. You wait, hoping
for the gift of my willingness
to acknowledge the good
you already see and the bad
you've long forgotten.

April 27

Lord, give me hope,
Give me patience to cope
And a reason to keep on trying.
Take my trembling hand
Give me power to stand
And a faith that is strong and undying.

September 15

Change is inevitable, Lord, I know. Help me to accept: If I view each transition as an opportunity to experience your faithfulness, I make new places in my life for spiritual growth.

April 28

When will the rain let up, Lord? Oh, soon: may your presence be to me as cleansing droplets of mercy, these clouds only filtering in glorious gold and purple the blazing rays of your grace.

September 14

Turn away mine eyes from beholding vanity;
and quicken thou me in thy way.

Psalm 119:37

Now therefore, our God, we thank thee,
and praise thy glorious name.

1 Chronicles 29:13

September 13

*F*orgive me, Lord, my sins, for failing to live up to your standards of goodness and justice. I confess my shortcomings. Make me willing to change and help me become a person of godly character. Amen.

April 30

Sometimes I feel abandoned, Lord. I feel empty inside, and it's hard to connect with myself, with others, and with the world. I almost lose faith at these times, Lord. Please stay with me and help me remember your love, your light, and your peace.

September 12

Your changes touch my life with hope and mystery. God of love and power, I come today ready and eager to experience your power working through me.

May 1

With clean hands and a pure heart, may I be worthy to do the work of angels.

Father, thank you for feathers and fur that cover the hearts of unexpected angels. Thanks for the softness between my fingers that reminds me of how my heart can grow. Thank you for the wonder they inspire, the smiles and laughter. Thank you for their touch and their ability to share. Everything that lives is holy, life delights in life.

William Blake, "America: A Prophesy"

May 2

I see a robin's egg hatching, Lord, and am set free from my doubts and fretting. For, while life is not always filled with joy and happiness, I know it is always held in your hand.

*Y*ou love me, Lord, not because I am particularly lovable. And it's certainly not the case that you need to receive my love. I am so heartened by this: You offer your love simply because you delight to do it.

May 3

$\mathcal{P}$lease be with me,
Lord, when pain strikes
me or those I love. Please
watch over me when my
body is stricken. Amen.

September 9

Examine me, O Lord, and prove me; try my reins and my heart. For thy lovingkindness is before mine eyes: and I have walked in thy truth.

Psalm 26:2–3

May 4

I accept your invitation to pray without ceasing. Hear me as I pray boldly, with expectation, believing your assurance that I deserve to be in your presence and to talk all I want. I am grateful that you welcome me at all times and in all places and moods.

September 8

$\mathcal{M}$any times I feel that I have the right to be downcast. But God's Word says that we should not be downcast because we have an amazing hope through him. If I focus on this hope, joy will enter my spirit, and my negative emotions will disperse.

May 5

$\mathcal{B}$lessed is that man that maketh the Lord
his trust, and respecteth not the proud,
nor such as turn aside to lies.

Psalm 40:4

September 7

The things, good Lord, that we pray for,
give us the grace to labour for.

St. Thomas More

May 6

Lord, I've tossed my prayers aloft, and hopefully, expectantly, I wait for your answers. As I do, I will: listen, for you to speak in the voice of nature; see you as a companion in the face and hand of a friend; feel you as a sweet-smelling rain, a river breeze; believe you can provide encouragement, direction, and guidance for those who have only to ask. I feel your presence.

September 6

*H*elp me be open to your guidance, Lord, however it comes. When you speak to me in the words of a friend, open my ears. When you touch me in the embrace of a family member, let me feel your gentle touch. Alert my senses to your presence at all times, Lord.

May 7

*L*ord, help me not accuse you of being untrue when I don't get from you everything I want, for you have promised to meet all my needs. And when I learn to love you supremely and trust you wholly, my desires will find fulfillment in you.

September 5

Lord, when I turn to you and trust you, you are very glad. Make me glad, too, as I learn to share your joy in finding what you lost. Amen.

May 8

$\mathcal{D}$ear God,
Drop thy still dews of quietness,
Till all our strivings cease;
Take from our souls the strain and stress,
And let our ordered lives confess
Thy beauty of thy peace.

John Greenleaf Whittier

September 4

Angels meet me coming and going. They cross my path. They walk by my side. They lead me and follow me and rise above me and pave the ground beneath me. They do whatever it takes to help me do the things God has called me to do.

May 9

Comfort me, God, when I come to this awesome conclusion: What did not satisfy me when I finally laid hold of it was surely not the thing I was so long in seeking. Yes, comfort me by this recognition: In all my longings, I am only yearning for you.

September 3

O Lord God of hosts, who is a strong Lord like unto thee? or to thy faithfulness round about thee?

Psalm 89:8

I am surprised by joy,
God of re-creation, when
I see despair outwitted
by simple acts of love as
small as grains of sand.
Keep me searching,
believing, and building
upon them, realizing that
grains of sand make dune,
shore, and desert.

Lord, once again I am aware that you, by your grace, gave me the strength to work through a situation that I was woefully unprepared to face. I accept that when I am completely out of ideas, drained of all energy, and so sick at heart I can barely breathe, your grace and strength lift me up and carry me forward. Thank you, Lord.

May 11

I acknowledge my sin unto thee, and mine iniquity have I not hid. I said, I will confess my transgressions unto the Lord; and thou forgavest the iniquity of my sin.

Psalm 32:5

September 1

God Almighty, thank you for the people that inspire me to accept others. Let me learn to love everyone— including myself. Amen.

May 12

$\mathcal{Y}$ou fulfilled this promise, Lord, when you gave your Holy Spirit to live within those who dedicate their lives to you. Thank you for transforming my heart with your saving grace and for making me sensitive to your Word and your ways. You truly have brought my soul alive—as if from stone to living flesh.

August 31

*H*eavenly Father, when you sent Jesus, you gave your best to this world. As I consider how to emulate that kind of love, I'd like to give in a significant way to someone in need. There are so many opportunities to give, but I'd like to do more than just buy a present. I'd like to give myself.

May 13

*E*ven in my toughest
moments, Lord, I yearn to
grow into the fullest flower.
Give me a faith as resilient
and determined as dandelions
pushing up through cracks
in the pavement.

God of All Comfort, I know that with you by my side I am never alone. Your perfect love casts out all fear, doubt, and uncertainty. Your presence emboldens and empowers me. You are the light that leads me to safety again. Amen.

$\mathcal{G}$od, you understand it all. You know what I feel. You ache with me. After all, your Son died in pain—nailed to a cross.

I know thee, who hast kept my path, and made
Light for me in darkness, tempering sorrow
So that it reached me like a solemn joy;
It were too strange that I should doubt thy love.

Robert Browning, "Paracelsus"

May 15

$\mathcal{T}$oday I'll simply trust you, Father. I'll remember that you're not looking for résumés full of impressive credentials; rather, you seek hearts that trust in you. You want to enjoy a vibrant, meaningful relationship with me—a relationship in which I trust you fully. That's the starting point of a life lived for you.

I don't want to do it all today, Lord. I want to leave undone that which fails to serve you, and leave unsaid that which fails to glorify you.

May 16

I can't make a blade of grass grow,
Lord. By contrast, you created this entire
universe and all it contains. If that doesn't
inspire worship in my soul, I can't imagine
what will. But the truth is that it does put
me in awe of you; it does stir my heart to
join in the worship of heaven.

August 27

*H*ave mercy upon me, O God, according to thy lovingkindness: according unto the multitude of thy tender mercies blot out my transgressions.

Psalm 51:1

May 17

Remember me, O Lord, with the favour that thou bearest unto thy people: O visit me with thy salvation; That I may see the good of thy chosen, that I may rejoice in the gladness of thy nation, that I may glory with thine inheritance.

Psalm 106:4–5

August 26

Thank you, God of inspiration, for the times when you guide me to take my place as an example and a model for others. For you call me to be loving, tender, and kind.

May 18

So many things will offer themselves to me for "worship" today. But reveal yourself, God, in all your creativity, as the only being worthy of my true adoration.

August 25

𝓡emove far from me vanity and lies: give me neither poverty nor riches; feed me with food convenient for me.

Proverbs 30:8

May 19

Lord Jesus, you are medicine to me when I am sick, strength to me when I need help, life itself when I fear death, the way when I long for heaven, the light when all is dark, and food when I need nourishment. Glory be to you forever. Amen.

St. Ambrose

*D*ear God, no one understands my suffering, but you do, for you know my heart even better than I do. Help me to walk through this dark valley of my pain and guide me back to the light of truth. I know that I am precious, but I don't feel that way right now. Help me see the reality of who I am—the magnificent creation you intended me to be. Amen.

May 20

Lord, I can hear your voice in the bubbling brook, see your beauty in the petals of a flower, and feel your gentle breath in the evening breeze and in the soft kiss of a child. Thank you for all of these gifts.

August 23

Father God, as I journey through life, remind me of your presence. Let me see your love in everything. Amen.

May 21

$\mathcal{F}$or he shall give his angels charge over thee,
to keep thee in all thy ways.

Psalm 91:11

Lord, I want my love for you to be expressed as naturally as breathing in and out. In that way my whole existence—my very life itself—will be an expression of my love for you. Accept my meager attempts to love you completely, Lord.

God, please remind me throughout my day that the moment is all I have in which to live. I can't retrieve or retract anything I've done or said just ten minutes ago. Nor can I be sure of what will happen ten minutes hence. So I pray, Lord, help me leave the past and the future with you so that I can experience the peace of your love in this important bit of eternity called "now."

O Lord, how grateful I am that, because of your love for me, you have cleansed me of my sin and offered me the gifts of forgiveness and salvation with open arms. Never fail to nudge me when I am starting down the wrong path, Lord. I know your corrections are better than the world's consequences.

May 23

*Y*ou are everywhere, Lord, and I am comforted to be enfolded as I move through life's extremes. You are with me in birthings and dyings, in routine and surprise, and in stillness and activity. I cannot wander so far in any direction that you are not already there.

August 20

O Lord, let me not live to be useless.

John Wesley

May 24

$\mathcal{I}$ delight to do thy will, O my God:
yea, thy law is within my heart.

Psalm 40:8

Lord,

In times of weakness and doubt, help me
remember that you are always capable of
miracles. Keep me ever alert to the possibility
of visits from your ministering angels
whom you send to protect and guide me.
May I receive them with a joyous and grateful
heart and then pass on the blessings to
others who need their comfort.

Amen.

May 25

Surrounded by a community of headstones, I remember, mourn, and celebrate, God of history and future. I feel grateful for the history written by strangers fallen in battle to insure my freedom-filled life of safety. I pause now to honor the efforts and accomplishments of ancestors. Bless those remembering, those remembered.

Lord, I pray I can find a place within my heart where I can let go of worries. I want to be filled with the calmness of a faith in you. Amen.

May 26

Commit thy way unto the Lord; trust also in him; and he shall bring it to pass.

Psalm 37:5

August 17

Mercy is not something
I need beg of you, O God,
for your pleasure is to love
me. Mercy, grace, and love
are always available to me,
Lord, for you are always
available to me.

May 27

God, I will try to learn and grow from challenges. I pray your promise of a new life can heal my wounds. I will try to remain patient because I know that you will cure me in good time. Amen.

August 16

God of all creatures, bless my pets, for they bless me, even when they shed on the couch and don't come when called. They love without strings and share the simplest joys of walks and catnaps, slowing me to a pace you recommend.

May 28

$\mathcal{F}$ather, instill in me the gifts of humor and joy. Teach me how to lift downcast spirits and dispense the medicine of good cheer in your name.

August 15

Be of good courage, and he shall strengthen your heart, all ye that hope in the Lord.

Psalm 31:24

May 29

$\mathcal{L}$ord, please bring this
truth home to my heart
today: that the essence of God
is love—your love reaching us
and setting our hearts aglow
with love for you and for all
people. Let love rule this day.
Let love rule my heart. Help
me enjoy living successfully
in your wonderful love.

August 14

*L*ike a child with pail
and shovel trying to
empty the ocean into
a hole dug in the sand,
O God, I can't begin to
fathom the enormity of
the love with which
you long to fill me.

May 30

All praise to Him who now hath turned
My fears to joys, my sighs to song,
My tears to smiles, my sad to glad. Amen.

Anne Bradstreet

August 13

Deliver me, O God, from a slothful mind, from all lukewarmness, and all dejection of spirit. I know these cannot but deaden my love to you; mercifully free my heart from them, and give me a lively, zealous, active, and cheerful spirit, that I may vigorously perform whatever you command, thankfully suffer whatever you choose for me, and be ever ardent to obey in all things your holy love.

John Wesley

May 31

Those people who are unlikable to me, Lord, are not worthless, though I'm tempted to believe my self-centered thoughts about them. Rather, Lord, these people are precious works of beauty, created by you. And if I bother to look beyond my first impressions, I will be delighted by what I see of you in them.

August 12

Why, O God, do bad things happen? Can I be angry when I pray? It's all I have to offer. I find relief sharing it with you; for now, that's all I need.

June 1

*T*end to me, loving Creator, and shelter me in the palm of Your hand.

August 11

There is plenty of evidence for the existence of God, but if one could absolutely prove it, faith wouldn't be necessary. Even with all the evidence of creation and the soul, God left room for us to be free beings. Freedom is what brings such creativity, invention, and interest to the world.

June 2

And blessed be his
glorious name for ever:
and let the whole earth
be filled with his glory;
Amen, and Amen.

Psalm 72:19

August 10

When I struggle in unfamiliar territory, Lord, I feel your calming, guiding hand and remember that you have always been faithful to your children. Then I know that my journey is safe. Please continue to give me confidence as I move to where you are calling.

You don't need to have perfect pitch to sing praises to God. Many worshippers take great comfort in the psalmist's mandate to make a joyful noise to the Lord. Joyful noises from attuned hearts are music to God's ears.

August 9

When I think about your example of love, dear God, I realize that love is far more than a warm emotion. It is a deep commitment to look out for another's best interest, even at my own expense. Please teach me to put my pride and my heart on the line. Please protect me, Lord, as I love others in your name. Amen.

June 4

It's amazing, steadfast God, how much better I feel after sharing with you even the smallest doubt or little worry. Connected, we can do great things. Alone, I am the victim of my own fears.

August 8

I will praise thee; for I am fearfully and wonderfully made: marvellous are thy works; and that my soul knoweth right well.

Psalm 139:14

June 5

Teach me, teach me, dearest Jesus
In thine own sweet, loving way,
All the lessons of perfection
I must practice day by day.
Teach me Meekness, dearest Jesus,
Of Thine own the counterpart;
Not in words and actions only,
But the meekness of the heart.
Teach Humility, sweet Jesus,
To this poor, proud heart of mine,
Which yet wishes, O my Jesus,
To be modeled after Thine.

Reverend F. X. Lasance

August 7

*L*ord, I looked at a recent problem from every angle imaginable, but it wasn't until I filtered it through your Word that the gems of wisdom and understanding appeared. How lost I would be without your guidance, Lord, and how blessed I am to have your counsel.

June 6

Lord, I come to you boldly and gladly. Accept me as your child, and meet my needs. Amen.

August 6

A faithful man shall abound with blessings.

Proverbs 28:20

June 7

For thou art my lamp, O Lord:
and the Lord will lighten my darkness.

2 Samuel 22:29

August 5

Lord, help me remember that you are the God of hope. You don't want me to feel sad or hopeless. It isn't your plan for me to live in fear or doubt. Help me to feel and access the power of the Holy Spirit. I know that through your Spirit I will find the hope and joy and peace you have promised to your people.

June 8

I'm getting a crick in my neck trying to see around the bend, God of past and future. I'm wearing myself out second guessing. Teach me to live in today, needing just a small glimpse down the road. No need to borrow trouble that may not be waiting.

August 4

Lord, dismiss us with thy blessing,
Hope, and comfort from above;
Let us each, thy peace possessing,
Triumph in redeeming love.

Robert Hawker

June 9

Enter and bless my
family, Lord, so that
its circle will be where
quarrels are made
up and relationships
mature, where failures
are forgiven and new
direction found.

August 3

How good it is, Almighty One, to bask in the warmth of your love. To know nothing more is required than this: receive your good gifts from above.

June 10

Holy God, you have shown me light and life. You are stronger than any natural power. Accept the words from my heart that struggle to reach you. Accept the silent thoughts and feelings that are offered to you. Clear my mind of the clutter of useless facts. Bend down to me, and lift me in your arms. Make me holy as you are holy. Give me a voice to sing of your love to others.

August 2

Lord, focusing on your Word is a great blessing. The more I keep it before me, the more faithfully I walk in your ways. Help me to make the most of every opportunity I have to read, think about, and discuss the things you share with us through the Scriptures.

June 11

$\mathscr{P}$reserve me, O God: for in thee do I put my trust.

Psalm 16:1

August 1

Lord, I'm glad that the more I give, you give. Reward me for the risks I take on your behalf. Amen.

June 12

We thank you, God,
for the moments of fulfillment:
the end of a day's work,
the harvest of sugar cane,
the birth of a child,
for in these pauses
we feel the rhythm
of the eternal.

Hawaiian Prayer

July 31

*I*n this beautiful place, there are wonders all around me, God, I know. The only thing lacking is wonder. Lift up my heart in praise!

June 13

Thank you, God of inspiration, for the times when you guide me to take my place as an example and a model for others.

July 30

Give me eyes, O God, to take a second look at those who think, act, and look different from me. Help me take seriously your image of them. Equip me with acceptance and courage as I hold out a welcoming hand, knowing that you are where strangers' hands meet.

Teach me to know, God, that it is exactly at the point of my deepest despair that you are closest. For at those times I can finally admit I have wandered in the dark, without a clue. Yet you have been there with me all along. Thank you for your abiding presence.

July 29

$\mathcal{B}$e thou exalted, O God, above the heavens:
and thy glory above all the earth.

Psalm 108:5

June 15

*F*ather, it's to you we come,
To pray for loved ones and for friends;
You offer mercy, grace, and peace,
And healing love that never ends.

July 28

*H*ow lovely, God, the newness of the life around me. Flower buds peek out from so many places. It's easy to imagine an angel behind every one breathing life and sending good energy to the world. Give me eyes to see. Give me a heart to respond.

June 16

Lord, help me to depend on you to be my source of goodness. I don't always feel like being patient, kind, loving, or joyful, but you are all of these things by your very nature. So right now I place my strengths and weaknesses into your hands, asking you to infuse them with yourself and to make them instruments of good that will serve others for your sake.

July 27

No matter the worries I have, small or large, you, O God, are there ahead of me with promises of help and support that relieve me and free me from getting stuck in the mire of my fear. I am grateful.

June 17

Create in me a clean heart, O God; and
renew a right spirit within me.

Psalm 51:10

July 26

Breathe in me, O Holy Spirit, that my thoughts may all be holy. Act in me, O Holy Spirit, that my work, too, may be holy. Draw my heart, O Holy Spirit, that I love but what is holy. Strengthen me, O Holy Spirit, to defend all that is holy. Guard me, then, O Holy Spirit, that I always may be holy. Amen.

St. Augustine

June 18

$\mathcal{Y}$ou think of everything, Lord God. I am often baffled by how to care for the most vulnerable among us, but your solution is simple: When you go to gather the fruits of your labor, leave something behind! Once I have what I need, it should be easy to leave the rest for others.

July 25

$\mathcal{B}$ut I am like a green olive tree in the house of God:
I trust in the mercy of God for ever and ever.

Psalm 52:8

June 19

I always want to be a dreamer, O God, to feel the stir and the yearning to see my vision become reality. There are those who would say dreamers are free-floaters. When I dream I feel connected to you and to your creation, bound by purpose and a sense of call. Nourish my dreams and my striving to make them real.

July 24

When the difficulties of daily life threaten to derail me, restore my peace of mind. Help me feel your strength within me so that I can tackle whatever difficulties come my way.

June 20

Grant, O Lord, that we may live in thy fear, die in thy favour, rest in thy peace, rise in thy power, reign in thy glory.

William Laud

July 23

Our Father, remind
me that to live a life of
faith is to live always
in your presence, at
peace in the home of
your love. Amen.

June 21

$\mathcal{S}$ometimes doing the right thing takes more guts than I'm able to muster, Lord. If I do what I know I should, people might get angry or exclude me. Help me, Lord! Give me the strength of character to follow you, even when it makes me unpopular for a while. I entrust the end result to you.

July 22

I am still moving, God, through storms. By your grace—over rough country, you have carried me; amidst pounding waves, you have held me; beyond the horizon of my longings you have shown me your purposes. Even in this small room, sitting still, I am moving, God. Closer.

June 22

*J*ust as you do not reject me or deny me love, O God, I should not reject or deny love from those around me. My love has the power to heal and influence others. May I use that power wisely.

July 21

Many, O Lord my God, are thy wonderful works which thou hast done, and thy thoughts which are to us-ward: they cannot be reckoned up in order unto thee: if I would declare and speak of them, they are more than can be numbered.

Psalm 40:5

June 23

Lord, I am thankful every day that you sent your Son to live among us. How blessed we are that he taught us about you and gave us such a beautiful example to follow. May I remember every day to pause and give thanks for this, so I do not get too caught up in my trivial, worldly cares.

July 20

Father, make me resilient like the sandy beach upon which the waves crash. Make me strong like the mighty willow tree that bends but does not break in the high winds. Give me the patience and wisdom to know that my suffering will one day turn to a greater understanding of your ways, your works, and your wonders.

June 24

Restore unto me the joy of thy salvation;
and uphold me with thy free spirit.

Psalm 51:12

July 19

Thank you, Lord, for helping me through hard times. You have shown your love for me and made me a more compassionate person. Help me show the same love to others who are going through hard times.

June 25

$\mathcal{B}$less these next few, short moments in my day before the next problem arises. And may I remember, in all my busyness, that the best time to seek you is always the same: now, right now.

July 18

Blessed are the meek: for they shall inherit the earth.

Matthew 5:5

As I learn to trust you, God, I discover your strengthening presence in various places and people. Wherever I encounter shelter, comfort, rest, and peace, I am bound to hear your voice, welcoming me. And in whomever I find truth, love, gentleness, and humility, I am sure to hear your heartbeat, assuring mc that you will always be near. Thank you, God. Amen.

July 17

I remember it—coming from a swim and lying back in white sand—the gift of a moment to rest, to sit in reverie, to watch, to close eyes and think of nothing but the sound of breaking waves. Yes, You were there with the sounds and the sunshine, and I am thankful.

June 27

The Lord bless thee, and keep thee: The Lord make his face shine upon thee, and be gracious unto thee: The Lord lift up his countenance upon thee, and give thee peace.

Numbers 6:24–26

July 16

Ye are the light of the world.
A city that is set on an hill cannot be hid.

Matthew 5:14

June 28

God, you are invisible but not unseen. You reveal yourself in creation and demonstrate your kindness in a stranger's sincere smile. You are intangible but not unfelt. You caress my face with the wind and embrace me in a friend's arms. I look for you and feel your presence. Amen.

July 15

Lord, I need you here in the midst of this difficult situation, that the very warmth of your love will bring about the resolution and that the brightness of your light will cast out all shadows between us. Amen.

June 29

Teach me to feel another's woe,
To hide the fault I see;
That mercy I to others show,
That mercy show to me.

Alexander Pope

July 14

Lord, just as the Jews and Gentiles were all presented the path leading to you, so are all those in the world today. Search our hearts, Lord. Don't let petty disagreements and differences of opinion lead us astray. We are so lost without you, Lord. Thank you for your open invitation to us all.

June 30

Lord, many times I have asked you to protect my heart from wanton wanderings, and you have always aided me. How grateful I am for your help, Lord. Thank you for steering my heart toward only what is good and true. My heart is full of love for many people, but it only belongs to you.

July 13

In thee, O Lord, do I put my trust: let me never be put to confusion.

Psalm 71:1

July 1

You listen as a hearer of my heart. And this is a moment to remind myself: Prayers have never needed words.

July 12

Lord, since you exist, we exist. Since you are beautiful, we are beautiful. Since you are good, we are good. By our existence we honour you. By our beauty we glorify you. By our goodness we love you.

Edmund of Abingdon

July 9

Give ear to my words, O Lord, consider my meditation.

Psalm 5:1

July 4

$\mathcal{L}$ord, how blessed I am to live in a country where I am free to worship as I please. Help me to never take such freedom for granted. On this Independence Day, I ask you to bless any believers who are being persecuted for living out their faith. Draw especially near to them, Lord. Surround them with your mighty army of angels.

July 10

Lord, my heart overflows with gratitude for all the blessings you have sent into my life. I am cognizant of the fact that I am probably only aware of a small percentage of them, though. You are such a generous God; you shower us with such abundance. I am grateful for it all, Lord.

July 3

O God, my heart is fixed;
I will sing and give praise, even with my glory.

Psalm 108:1

July 11

Lord, your word created all there
is. Let it now create a powerful
restoration within me. Your love
sustains all life. Let it now sustain and
renew me. Your strength holds up the
galaxies. Let it now hold me up and
give me support. Your light reaches the
far ends of the universe. Let it shine its
healing energy upon me now. Amen.

July 2

Thank you, God, that even when I fret, I know without a doubt that you are using my unique, special gifts and talents to nurture and teach my children. When I get down on myself and am unsure of my abilities, remind me that your commitment to me is lifelong.